T0355678

The Moon a Box

M.L. Liebler

New Issues Poetry & Prose

A Green Rose Book

New Issues Poetry & Prose
The College of Arts and Sciences
Western Michigan University
Kalamazoo, Michigan 49008

An Inland Seas Poetry Book

 Inland Seas poetry books are supported by a grant from
The Michigan Council for Arts and Cultural Affairs.

First Edition, 2004.

ISBN   1-930974-39-6 (paperbound)

Library of Congress Cataloging-in-Publication Data:
Liebler, M.L.
The Moon a Box/M.L. Liebler
Library of Congress Control Number: 2003116225

Editors	Eric Hansen, Jonathan Pugh, Herbert Scott
Art Director	Tricia Hennessy
Designer	Srey Pen
Production Manager	Paul Sizer
	The Design Center, Department of Art
	College of Fine Arts
	Western Michigan University

The Moon a Box

M.L. Liebler

New Issues

WESTERN MICHIGAN UNIVERSITY

Also by M.L. Liebler

A Moment of Understanding: The China Poems

Breaking the Voodoo & Other Poems

Written In Rain: New & Selected Poems 1985-2000

Brooding the Heartlands: Poems of the Midwest

Stripping the Adult Century Bare

Working Words: Labor & Working Class Literature (Editor)

Abandon Automobile: Detroit City Poetry (Co-Editor)

Northern Lights: Poetry from Northern Michigan University
   (Editor)

Recordings

Crossing Borders (with Country Joe McDonald)

Paper Ghost Raindance (with The Magic Poetry Band)

The Gift Outright (with The Magic Poetry Band)

Kickin' Game: Live in Prison (with The Magic Poetry Band)

Stick This Up: Poems in Performance (with special guests)

Breaking the Voodoo & Other Performance Poems
   (with special guests)

for Pamela M. Liebler,
  lifelong companion and very best friend

Darling, do you remember
The man you married? Touch me,
Remind me who I am.
                    —Stanley Kunitz

Contents

The moon was once a moth who ran to God,
they entwined.

—Rumi

I was born to rock the boat,
Some will sink, but we will float—
Grab your coat, let's get outta here.
You're my witness; I'm your mutineer.

—Warren Zevon

I.

Arctic Dream

Descending through the bruised blueness
Of fresh arctic sky, in these moments
Before landing, I am beginning to discover
A new self buried in the Inupiat earth,
Under centuries of ritual and prayer.

I am again looking for answers to questions
That seem to reach across the tundra
As far as the eye can see. I am learning
The ancient art of rhythm and balance.

The wind is a new truth.
It changes like the sun's position
In the midnight sky,
Horizon hurrying west, never
To find dusk at the earth's edge.

Barrow, AK

M.L. to Himself

Above the broken
Rocks of an earthquake
I gaze at beauty

As it was intended,
The geography I have craved
All my life.

The mountain settles—
A certain unknowable moment—
In quiet meditation,

Returning itself to beauty.
The ancient beginnings, again—
As they once were.

Anchorage, AK

Arctic Heart

North of the Arctic Circle,
West of my life, atop
The snow and the ancient ice,
In the ocean's wind and salt I find grace.

Here—everything from walrus
Ivory to the bowhead whale's
Icy heart keep our futures warm
In the blueness of this fresh world.

Barrow, AK

Downbeat Blue

Each chord struck
Sends the earth scattering
From bare bone, blue
Downbeat into the thin
Layers of rock and mud.

Fairbanks, AK

In Eek

All alone in Eek,
I am no more
Than a breeze from
The Bering Sea
Coastline of walrus tusk,
Seal fur, fresh whale oil.

I sit watching
Nothing at all.

No work here in Eek,
No money, and all
The time in the world
To sit and think about nothing.

Eek, AK

How Small the News

Arriving late, on Alaskan time,
A message is translated from bubbles
That rise up through the tundra waters,
And again over the quiet riverbanks—
Current of a small, good news.

How small the news was,
Coming north up the Kuskoswim
River from Good News Bay. Words
Traveling slower than silt over
Riverbeds, coaxing secrets
From the sleepy salmon.

Bethel, AK

Inland Waters

Like so many icebound fish,
My dreams lie awake.

A twilight comet shoots through
The Arctic Circle—life and snow.

Such tiny mercies we miss daily
As they slide past our pain like tenderness,

So many unknown stars
Slipping through the galaxy.

Earthquake Park, AK

Rising Up From

Here I, again, catch myself
Passing myself. Tonight
The sun will burn
Throughout the day
And well past midnight.

The sun's mist of kindness
Rises up from iceberg fog—
A dream hiding quietly just below.
Today I catch myself
Catching the morning light

On the very tip of my tongue.
I am waiting and waiting for eternity
In the leaves of a single tundra
Flower. Always it has been there,
Alone and alive in the cold
Northern underbrush.

Point Barrow, AK

II.

Twilight Blues

The twilight blues descend
Upon the neon snake.
Electric city signs
Ongoing and going
On. A language spoken in miles.
Road after all the other
Roads. It's another
Angel's wing waving
Goodbye to

Our city—broken spirits.
Spent confusion. Every-
Where separate, not equal. And we
Live here. Nobody sayin' nothing,
Turning blind eyes like double
Plays. Dust, bottles, make-up.
Blue jazz wailing thru
Thin breeze on the eights.
It's ghosts. Birds.
They live
      here
         now!

Detroit, MI

The Science of Racism

What cradles the river
Cradles me.
　　　　　　—Judith Roche

I died when I was born.
We were all dropped darkly
Through a thermal test tube
In the name of
The American spirit, in which
Cells divide and separate as easy
As oil and water, black and white.

There's some type of disturbing science
At work here, where
Generations thrive and climb
Down horizons of salt and silt.
They are filled with tears—won't ever break
Free from history, destiny.

Is it endless—
Cycle of entropy, birth
To death? Another broken
Promise? Ignorance buried
Within unyielding hearts, in
The name of God, of country?

Detroit, MI

The Order of Terror

—for Larry Scaff

In our lives, there are time
Zones in which even suicide
Is no escape. At every turn, violence
Seems to open us with a cutting
Vapor that streams through
The essence of our terror. It leaves
Us powerless and disoriented.
We are abandoned at the core.

An emptiness, like tomorrow, licks
Us dry at the point when we can no longer
Tell the difference between the oil
Of ourselves and the randomness
Of our conscience. We choose death
Over prayer, sin over life.

Detroit, MI

The Undertow

From the undertow,
The swirling blood
Of envy flowed—

Drained my body
Pale and dry
Upon the bone

Earth, my death.
I fascinated myself
Within the skin

Of my darkness.
I stood alone,
Believing no one—

Understanding my future
Less and less.
A shadow against
The moon's face.

Springfield, MA

May 4th

—after 30 years, Kent State

Thirty years ago
This very day, fate,
Like a breaking bottle,
Hit the empty cement
Of an American street.
The howl of
A generation
Set the world ajar,
Tumbled through
Loss and fury.

If we wake tomorrow
This dream will be
Our national nightmare.
We will know
It as our fortune, read
Aloud by a tragic teller of
Things to come, and soon.

Costa Mesa, CA

My Sin

If I know my angels,
I know what they would say
                              —Joe Henry

He came to me
In a whisky-blue dream
In midtown Manhattan.

He wasn't angry anymore.
He seemed happy to find
Me again, my old self.

Picking up his ghost guitar,
He played me a new song.
He played it innocent and sweet

As if he were the world's only child,
His whole future ahead,
No pain hidden in that past.

In some undeserved way, I felt
As though he had forgiven me
For the hurtfulness of my words.

His kindness to me was more
Genuine than all of my love could
Ever have been toward him.

In my dream, I found myself running
Back and forth in search of forgiveness,
In search of something greater.

But each time I was returned
To wander out my sin in prayer—
The sleepless turmoil of my penance
Revealed and served.

New York, NY

The Sadness of Things

No sadness but in things
                    —after W.C.W.

All alone and on my back, I hear
The soft buzz of a hummingbird's
Wing, close now to the honey.
Shoreline of my heart: I feel my way

Around the hollow of its echo.
I use this sound as my compass,
Navigate each tightening fiber
In my body. I am alive as long

As I am, but the invisible heart
Slows with sleep until
I am lost in the sad trees of my youth.
Once I saw myself as a lonely
Child swinging—in another dream,

Long before I was conceived.
I hid behind the pain of this
World's expectations. Later I
Was caught in its everydayness.

Now in my unforgiveness I am
Free to walk where I will—free
To move one more step away
From the dark clouds inside me.

Boyne Falls, MI

The Trick

She didn't say much.
It was a trick,
Just another lullaby to persuade
Me to close the darkness
Around me.

It was her memory that opened
And closed within the music box.
I was left to sing the old songs
With her, in the back yard.

She said: "The blind can't hide
Behind facial expressions because they
Have never seen them." It is
A miracle that we choose to hide behind
The sunshine—new light
Splashed upon our dreams.

Beside her, on a table:
The Lord's Prayer, Chinese tattoos,
A cross bearing a collage of all
Her children.

In the end, though, she only desired
To crawl back into her mother's bed,
To die within the silence.
Another shadow behind
The blood, in the emptiness.

Detroit, MI

Worn Edges

—for Debi Allen Faulkner

He needed a passport.
It was Canada, 1942.
He felt the need to see
His only child, whom he didn't
Know. The edges of his life
Dusty and ragged, bent by too much
History, by self-inflicted pain.
His pale blue
Eyes like translucent fish
In the night stream.

He lived alone, as a farmer,
For many years hoping to grow
A life that meant more than it seemed.
In the end, he became a master
Of clocks. He could never turn back
Time to save himself from the barren
Fields he had cultivated alone—
A world of eternal dirt and ash.

St. Clair Shores, MI

III.

Breaking the Voodoo

I better think about this.
Something is happening
To me because
Something is rattling
Inside of me
To move my spirit up
Through the top
Of my bald head,
And it's hot!
It's like a volcano burning
Somewhere between my soul
And my pancreas,
And I gotta ride it
Up through my stomach,
Past my emotions.
Quick!
Light some incense.
Place it on the altar of my shoulders.
Fan the flames.
This might take awhile.
Get more incense to burn.
CHANT/CHANT/CHANT.
Get the goat.
If not the goat, how
About some more incense?
Fan the flame.
Rip the fur.
Blow the blood.
I'm—I'm
Breaking the voodoo.
Tonight's the night.
I'm breaking the voodoo
The voodoo on everything.
I'm breaking the voodoo
On McDonald's secret sauce,
The one that killed
That lady up in Montreal in '78.

I'm breaking the voodoo
On all secret negotiations
With saucy countries
That should really be given the secret sauce
Instead of secret weapons and such.
Furthermore, I'm breaking the voodoo
On all families that supply
Saucy countries with children.
May they all experience the secret sauce!
Look what happened in Montreal!

I'm breaking the voodoo
On religion, as it were.
I'm breaking the voodoo
That says to be a good Christian
You have to support Jim & Tammy
Or Robertson & Tilton
Or Jerry & Orel
Or John & Paul.
And while I'm on the subject
I'm breaking the voodoo
On rock groups of the '60s
that still tour
As John, Paul, George, & Ringo
Didn't!
While I'm at it and
In the same stanza,
I'm breaking the voodoo
On Mark David Chapman.
Although I'm several years late,
He is broken and, therefore,
Forgiven.

In fact, I'm breaking the voodoo
On *all* past, present and future ass ass ins.
Let's keep it all in perspective.
Keep your business with politicians!

And I'm breaking the voodoo
On politicians, so they won't
Have to be the victims of assassins.
(Stop pitting folks against each other
To lie for you
And people won't need to send assassins
To kill you,
So much.)
I'm breaking the voodoo
On the KKK.
Start doing the right thing
Under those sheets, boys.

I'm breaking the voodoo
On all poets and artists
Who think their art
Is such a statement
They don't have
To speak the L-A-N-G-U-A-G-E.

I'm breaking the voodoo
On all warring nations.
Listen to your souls
And pray to your gods.
And if nothing happens,
So what!
At least you will not have killed
Anyone in the time you spent
In prayer and meditation.

Now I'll break the voodoo
On all body counts.
I also break the voodoo
On arithmetic.
There! Now you can't count!

I break the voodoo
On punks.
I wouldn't mind them
If I could trust them—
Skinheaded-
Purple-mohawk-haired-eyebrow-pierced
Kids—not to vote Republican.
But since I can't trust them
I break their voodoo.

I break the voodoo
On all Newt, Limbaugh, Engler types.
And all other fat-ass-Republican-
Weightwatcher-dropout-pennyloafer-
Wearin'-bleeding-madras-shirted-Docker-
Panted turd stubs.
Let them go without food and shelter
And the pursuit of happiness blah, blah, blah.
Just one day—let's see how well they do as
Pandhandlin', street-beggin', soup-kitchen constituents.

I break the voodoo
On Michigan-/Montana-/Idaho-Militia people
And all those play-soldier-paintball-shootin'
Survivalist bastards who have
More in common with my cheese-dick-
Racist-bigot-macho-mouthed-retired-
White-Detroit-Police-officer neighbor than with
The Black Panthers,
Weathermen Underground,
Sandinistas.

I break the voodoo
On all older women who forgot
To take their calcium when they were young.
Straighten up!
Straighten up!
You're *free*.

I break the voodoo
On the oppression-suppression-
repression of all women.
Let them up, off, and out
To be free
In a world that owes them
Everything
And fears to give them anything.

I break the voodoo
On public machoismoism,
On all those guys
Who drive around with no
Shirts, and hang out car windows screamin'
To impress women.

Finally, I break the voodoo
On cheap, self-absorbed people
Who hold paper and coin
In such high regard
That they'd let
Their brothers & sisters starve
So they can buy
The big burgers
With the secret sauce
That killed the lady
In Montreal
In '78.

I break the voodoo!
I break the voodoo!!
I break the VOODOO!!!
On it all
On it ALL
ON IT ALL
TONIGHT!

IV.

Pitchin' Shoes

I must be mad
Tonight. I must be
Drunk. Running out
In half circles
To the boat house
To stand on top of the day-
Warmed shingles and
Transform myself
Into a giant conch shell.

I'm going to build
My energy level up
High and let my vision
Whine out like steam.

I'm looking for,
And going to find,
Everything!

Tonight, I promise.

Out there in the dark
I'll come to terms,
And balance the universe
On the fulcrum of my soul.

Out there in the dark
Someone's pitchin' horseshoes
Around golden stakes,
Waiting for me,
Knowing I will change
From man to howling conch.
And like the horseshoe stars,
I will fall to the horizon,
Create
Two more stars
To ring the darkness.
The way it is.

Rochester, MI

Who Walked the Line

At the end
Of my brooding
Hallway, a memory.

My grandfather's jacket—
Blue and plaid, hung
Slightly off-kilter
On the old brass coat rack.

It is stained and wrinkled by the
Life that filled his full heart.

This was the jacket of a simple man
Who walked through
Factory soot and noise—
Thirty-odd years, the assembly line.

My grandfather's jacket hangs
Alone and unadorned like
A quiet life. It is honored
And dignified by his years
Of hard work, his loyalty.

Walloon Lake, MI

I Lost Long Ago Beside

—for Al Kooper

Last night, in the East,
I found something I thought
I had lost long ago beside a river.
My native tongue swam
Upstream, more alive than ever.
(It came to me as a Rainbow
Trout in my dream.) Bearing no scars,
It welcomed me back into a new
Translation of another America,
Where language was more
Than just another flag. My native tongue
Whispered to me, sometime
Close to 6:00am, that I have never been
As far away from myself as I once thought.
With new breath, I took one more look
At the water. I decoded
My future into this new language,
The language I never really lost.

Boston, MA

Rock 'n' Roll

My grandma taught me
How to rock.
She hummed Elvis
While she hemmed my pants.
She liked Elvis.
She liked him so much
That she bought me
A black leather jacket
With zippers, and a motorcycle hat
—Like Marlon Brando's—
That really pissed Mrs Taylor off!
She kicked me out of first grade.
She said I'd be a bad influence
On all the other kids.

Ah—I didn't like those snotty-nosed kids
        anyway.
They couldn't rock
Like grandma.

St. Clair Shores, MI

Humidity Falling

—for Clitha & Lynne

Humidity fell from the willow trees
Onto my brow. Just as quick
It slid into the stream, slid
Into Cape Fear River.

Deep in the South, where
Rum nights fold into heat
And sugarcane, the backwater
Swamps boil:

Reminder of our ghost selves
Standing just outside the door of the old
Slave Market House.

It's living with the law
That brings us to the brink
Of death, and it's our
Collective fear that denies
Us faith and freedom.

Old South, another
American tombstone.
We are called to stand trial
For our history and our shame.

Fayetteville, NC

Blue Alone

You must change your life.
   —Rilke

Inside my blue
Anxiety: swirling
Light of indecision,
Chaos turning
In dark shadows.
It pulls me closer
To what I least understand
About my loneliness.

What I want most is love
Delivered through every pore
Of my skin, inhaled
Through openness.

"Bring it closer!"
I'd say to my pulse.
"Bring it all in!"

Let me bathe in
The faith of tomorrow
While kissing tenderness
Off every single sharp-edged star.

I know now that I cannot
Stop everything everywhere.
But I believe I can stop
Some pain from sliding
Into my dreams while I lie
Awake in these summer
Nights, under sweat and clouds.

     New Orleans, LA

A Lonely Blues to Be

*—for Andrei, Brigitte, Laura
& Sally in the Alley, French Quarter, 2001*

Her heart is a globe
With hidden territories that
Could end all slavery.

She knew things
That were deeper
Than the muddy waters
Of the Mississippi Delta.

"There are some secrets,"
She said, "that can't be
Kept inside too long.
The southern river sun
Will dance them out from under us."

Now we are left to shake our mysteries
Like voodoo rainsticks,
And stones have settled atop
Our broke-luck selves.

She's my tarot, my tea leaf,
Good omen of luck lying in wait.
In the dark bayou I let this mud sing
Me to sleep—a lonely blues played
Against the face of the rising sun.

New Orleans, LA

V.

Southeast Asia, Coming Here

Coming here was no mistake
Call it my moment
My first opening
For the message that fell
Through the world
A new language to tell
I was welcome friend
And not blind enemy

Coming here
Was no mistake
A new truth offered
In warm rain
Breaking me open
Like sweet fruit
Fallen from a tree
Another life

Hong Kong, China

A Moment of Understanding

—for Shirley Geok-lin Lim

Yesterday, just under
Victoria Peak on Hong Kong
Island, I learned an important lesson
While listening to children play
Under the Asian sun.

It was as if God whispered
In the language of Zen:
"A dog's bark
Is a dog's bark and
Children's laughter
Is children's laughter;
This is enough
To know about the
Differences in this world."

Victoria Peak, China

The Blinding Road Blues

—after St. Paul

It was a hard road.
No one will ever
Understand that part
Of me—its journey
Down the winding streets
Of Pok Fu Lam.

Later I was to learn
That people were describing
Me as a loner, as alien.
But that was not the truth
I carried on my back
As an open letter
For the universe to read.

I remember being
Alone in a night
That filled me with sand
From an hourglass, and
Counted every doubt that ever
Crossed from one side
Of the South China
Sea back to the other.

Never before had I tempted
My midnight soul.
I found my heartbeat
Like a cloud within
My own desires,
Lifting up and over
The mountain's horizon.

It was you, sweet Asia,
The music and soul
Of Hong Kong, that pulled me
From twilight and brought me

Close, to where I could see my long
Escape from shaded loneliness.

Pok Fu Lam, China & Walloon Lake, MI

Green Mountain Morning

The white fog lifting
Off the top of a green
Mountain morning,

Lifting away
From the naked
Spirit to expose the lies
Of old prejudice,

Of mistaken identity
And cruel allegiance.

We pay for all our
Blindnesses double-time,
Backwards, in reverse.

China

Silence

The door closing
When there is no door.

Washington, D.C.

The Blue Wave

Yesterday I sat on
The ancient shoreline
Of the South China Sea.

I breathed deep—
The smell of mud, salt
And sand. I listened
To fishermen netting
Out in Stanley Bay.

Silence filled me with its
Big, blue wave. A swallowing
Peace I had never known.

Stanley Bay, China

Kowloon Night, Hong Kong Days

On Nathan Street,
The Chinese "Golden Mile,"
A young man, legless,
Bangs and bangs his tin cup
On the chipped cement sidewalk.

Moments like these
Fill my Kowloon nights and
Hong Kong days with the blood
Of a thousand miles, with
Broken pieces of loneliness.

Kowloon, China

Lost Sailor on The Big Muddy Pearl

> *You're a lost sailor*
> *Been way too long at sea*
> —Bob Weir

I have learned to be
At home in this world.
Even at those times when I lose
My way, I find
The Dog Star that hides
Behind the cow-jumped moon.

Sometimes I will forget which
Trade wind I hung my name upon,
Or where I left my soul, that lonely
Flag flapping in distress—a compass
To remind me to follow the road,
Follow its scrawl
Up the green mountain
And out over the Pearl River
Delta of Macau. It's there where I can
Breathe through the fanning mud and water
That rushes out toward Hong Kong Island,
Through the blue, primal night.
I am an old sailor drawn
To the horizon.

Macao, China

Which Stone We

—after Steven Schreiner

Where we go now
Depends upon which
Stone we sit upon
To see our future.

Somewhere within a universe
Of spirit and wind—
Our hidden address.

St. Louis, MO

Acknowledgments

I would like to sincerely thank all of the editors at the following journals, reviews and small presses, where many of these poems first appeared in similar or slightly different form:

Gary Metras at The Adastra Press, Jerry Kelly at The X0X0X Press, Mark Donovan at The Parkside Press, along with *Rattle: Poetry for the 21st Century Journal, The Paterson Literary Review, Exquisite Corpse, Yuan Yang: The University of Hong Kong Literary Review, University of Macao Poetry Review, Süddeutsche Zeitung: Munich,* and *Identity Lessons: Contemporary Literature About Learning to be American* (Viking-Penguin), edited by Maria Mazziotti Gillan.

Also, I would like to offer heartfelt thanks to Wanda Coleman and Herbert Scott for taking the time to help edit and make important suggestions about the poems in this manuscript.

Finally, I extend special thanks to Al Kooper, Vanessa & Jorma Kaukonen, Country Joe McDonald, Mike Watt & The Secondmen, Professor "Louie" and The Crowmatix, Robert B. Jones, Stewart Francke, Faruq Z. Bey, Alex Lumelsky, Jere Stormer, Stuart Tucker, Tom Feeney, Bill Boyer and all the members of The Magic Poetry Band (past & present) for their support, friendship and help in making the enclosed CD. This project was a true labor of love by all the musicians who so graciously gave of their time and talents.

CD Tracks, Credits and Acknowledgments

Unless otherwise noted, M.L. Liebler (www.mlliebler.com) is the author of, and vocalist on, *The Moon a Box*. Several special guest musicians performed with him:

1. Blue Alone (6:35)
Music © 2003 by Professor "Louie" & The Crowmatix, featuring Aaron "Professor 'Louie'" Hurowitz, Marie Spinosa, Gary Burke, Mike Dunn, Mike Demicco. Produced by Arron Hurowitz

2. A Lonely Blues To Be (1:17)
Music written, performed and produced by Al Kooper © 2002

3. The Undertow / Blood in the Moon (6:48)
Music © 2003 by Alex Lumelsky. Performed by The New Magic Poetry Band, featuring Faruq Z. Bey, Jere Stormer, Alex Lumelsky, Stuart Tucker & Tom Feeney. Produced by Alex Lumelsky, Jere Stormer & Adam Druckman

4. Brooding the Heartland (3:42)
Music written & performed by Ted Nagy, Jim Carey & Brigitte Knudson © Magic Poetry Band 2000. From the CD *Paper Ghost Raindance,* produced by Dean Western

5. The Blue Wave That Overcomes Us (1:10)
Music written, performed and produced by Al Kooper © 2002

6. Barren Tree Under Dark Sky (6:24)
Music written and performed by The Magic Poetry Trio, featuring Faruq Z. Bey, Alex Lumelsky & M.L. Liebler. Live Recording from the 2003 St. Louis Langston Hughes Black Arts Festival

7. The Lazarus Dream (3:46)
Music © 1997 by Bill Boyer. Performed by M.L. Liebler & The Magic Poetry Band, with Bill Boyer, Steve Bitto and Michael Smith. From the CD *The Gift Outright,* produced by Stephen "Leggy" Szajna

8. Lost Sailor On the Big Muddy Pearl (3:47)
Music © 2003 by Mike Watt. Performed by Mike Watt & The Secondmen. Produced by Mike Watt

9. The Blinding Road Blues (1:31)
Music written, performed and produced by Al Kooper © 2002

10. In Memory of the Passion Stars (7:06)
Music written by Matt Nikkari, Jim Carey, Tom Voiles and M.L. Liebler. © by, and performed by, M.L. Liebler & The Magic Poetry Band, from the CD *The Gift Outright,* produced by Stephen "Leggy" Szajna

11. Decoration Day (4:27)
The song "Remembrance" was written & performed by Country Joe
McDonald on the CD *Crossing Borders: The Poetry of M.L Liebler &*
The Music of Country Joe McDonald © 2002 by Alkatraz Corner Music Co.
for Rag Baby Records, Inc. Produced by Joe McDonald

12. Assassination (11:19)
Music written & performed by Robert B. Jones, Stewart Francke &
M.L. Liebler © 1997. Featuring Matt Nikkari on bass guitar, with voice
samples from John F. Kennedy, Martin Luther King, Jr., Robert Frost,
street scene in Chicago 1968, Mayor Richard Daley & Richard M. Nixon.
From the CD *The Gift Outright*, produced by Stephen "Leggy" Szajna

13. Who Walked the Line (3:31)
Music written & performed by Jorma Kaukonen © 1995 from his song "Do
Not Go Gentle," produced by Jorma Kaukonen and Michael Falzarano

14. I Lost Long Ago Beside (1:02)
Music written, performed and produced by Al Kooper © 2002

15. The Dream of Life (4:19)
Music © 1997 by William Boyer. Performed by Bill Blank & Dean Western.
From the CD *The Gift Outright*, produced by Stephen "Leggy" Szajna

16. Stick This Up (Hip Hop Demo Version) (3:02)
Music © 2003 by William Boyer. Performed by Bill Blank, produced by
Xander Sky

17. Worn Edges (1:02)
Music written, performed and produced by Al Kooper © 2002

18. The Moon a Box (0:46)
Music written, performed and produced by Al Kooper © 2002

**CD mastered by Adam Druckman for Drawing Room Studios in Detroit,
Michigan, 2003**

See below for information on all the artists who, in support of poetry, graciously appeared on this CD. Their time, treasures, talents and friendships are greatly appreciated by the author.

Al Kooper
www.alkooper.com

Jorma Kaukonen
www.hottuna.com www.jeffersonairplane.com www.furpeaceranch.com

Country Joe McDonald
www.countryjoe.com

Professor "Louie" & The Crowmatix
www.woodstockrecords.com

Robert B. Jones
www.robertbjones.com

Stewart Francke
www.blueboundary.com

Alex Lumelsky
www.xandersky.com

photo by Alex Lumelsky

M.L. Liebler has read and performed his poetry around the world at the Dodge Poetry Festival, Poetry Project of St. Mark's Church, Woody Guthrie Free Folk Festival, Annual Bumbershoot Arts Festival in Seattle, Hong Kong International Poetry Festival, Macao International Poetry Festival, London Poetry Society, University of Novosibirsk (Russia), the Substanz Slam Series in Munich, and in small villages throughout northern and western Alaska. He is the founding director of The YMCA National Writer's Voice Project in Detroit; the International Coordinator for the YMCA of USA's World YArts Initiative; and has taught literature, creative writing, American Studies and Labor Studies at Wayne State University since 1980.

New Issues Poetry & Prose

Editor, Herbert Scott

Vito Aiuto, *Self-Portrait as Jerry Quarry*
James Armstrong, *Monument In A Summer Hat*
Claire Bateman, *Clumsy*
Michael Burkard, *Pennsylvania Collection Agency*
Christopher Bursk, *Ovid at Fifteen*
Anthony Butts, *Fifth Season*
Anthony Butts, *Little Low Heaven*
Kevin Cantwell, *Something Black in the Green Part of Your Eye*
Gladys Cardiff, *A Bare Unpainted Table*
Kevin Clark, *In the Evening of No Warning*
Cynie Cory, *American Girl*
Jim Daniels, *Night with Drive-By Shooting Stars*
Joseph Featherstone, *Brace's Cove*
Lisa Fishman, *The Deep Heart's Core Is a Suitcase*
Robert Grunst, *The Smallest Bird in North America*
Paul Guest, *The Resurrection of the Body and the Ruin of the World*
Robert Haight, *Emergences and Spinner Falls*
Mark Halperin, *Time as Distance*
Myronn Hardy, *Approaching the Center*
Brian Henry, *Graft*
Edward Haworth Hoeppner, *Rain Through High Windows*
Cynthia Hogue, *Flux*
Christine Hume, *Alaskaphrenia*
Janet Kauffman, *Rot* (fiction)
Josie Kearns, *New Numbers*
Maurice Kilwein Guevara, *Autobiography of So-and-so: Poems in Prose*
Ruth Ellen Kocher, *When the Moon Knows You're Wandering*
Ruth Ellen Kocher, *One Girl Babylon*
Gerry LaFemina, *The Window Facing Winter*
Steve Langan, *Freezing*
Lance Larsen, *Erasable Walls*
David Dodd Lee, *Abrupt Rural*
David Dodd Lee, *Downsides of Fish Culture*
M.L. Liebler, *The Moon a Box*
Deanne Lundin, *The Ginseng Hunter's Notebook*
Joy Manesiotis, *They Sing to Her Bones*
Sarah Mangold, *Household Mechanics*
Gail Martin, *The Hourglass Heart*
David Marlatt, *A Hog Slaughtering Woman*
Louise Mathias, *Lark Apprentice*
Gretchen Mattox, *Buddha Box*
Gretchen Mattox, *Goodnight Architecture*

Paula McLain, *Less of Her*
Sarah Messer, *Bandit Letters*
Malena Mörling, *Ocean Avenue*
Julie Moulds, *The Woman with a Cubed Head*
Gerald Murnane, *The Plains* (fiction)
Marsha de la O, *Black Hope*
C. Mikal Oness, *Water Becomes Bone*
Elizabeth Powell, *The Republic of Self*
Margaret Rabb, *Granite Dives*
Rebecca Reynolds, *Daughter of the Hangnail; The Bovine Two-Step*
Martha Rhodes, *Perfect Disappearance*
Beth Roberts, *Brief Moral History in Blue*
John Rybicki, *Traveling at High Speeds* (expanded second edition)
Mary Ann Samyn, *Inside the Yellow Dress*
Ever Saskya, *The Porch is a Journey Different from the House*
Mark Scott, *Tactile Values*
Martha Serpas, *Côte Blanche*
Diane Seuss-Brakeman, *It Blows You Hollow*
Elaine Sexton, *Sleuth*
Marc Sheehan, *Greatest Hits*
Sarah Jane Smith, *No Thanks—and Other Stories* (fiction)
Phillip Sterling, *Mutual Shores*
Angela Sorby, *Distance Learning*
Russell Thorburn, *Approximate Desire*
Rodney Torreson, *A Breathable Light*
Robert VanderMolen, *Breath*
Martin Walls, *Small Human Detail in Care of National Trust*
Patricia Jabbeh Wesley, *Before the Palm Could Bloom: Poems of Africa*